MW01483501

The Blue Moth of Morning

P. C. VANDALL

The Blue Moth

of Morning

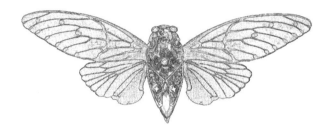

The Porcupine's Quill

Published by The Porcupine's Quill, 68 Main Street, PO Box 160, Erin, Ontario NOB 1TO. http://porcupinesquill.ca

Readied for the press by Stephanie Small.

Represented in Canada by Canadian Manda.
Trade orders are available from University of Toronto Press.

Library and Archives Canada Cataloguing in Publication

Title: The blue moth of morning / P.C. Vandall.
Names: Vandall, P.C., 1973– author.
Descripiton: Poems.
Identifiers: Canadiana 20200184407 | ISBN 9780889844339 (softcover)
Classification: LCC PS8643.A6875 B58 2020 | DDC C811/.6 — dc23

We acknowledge the support of the Ontario Arts Council and the Canada Council for the Arts for our publishing program. The financial support of the Government of Canada through the Canada Book Fund is also gratefully acknowledged.

Canada Council   Conseil des arts
for the Arts   du Canada

Canadä

ONTARIO ARTS COUNCIL
CONSEIL DES ARTS DE L'ONTARIO
an Ontario government agency
un organisme du gouvernement de l'Ontario

Ontario
Ontario Media Development
Corporation

For Derrick, Taylor and Ashlyn.

For Santa who gave me a typewriter
when I asked him for a computer.

To see a World in a Grain of Sand
And a Heaven in a Wild Flower
Hold infinity in the palm of your hand
And Eternity in an hour

—William Blake

Table of Contents

Stage Three: COCOON

Stage Four: MOTH

In memory of Alex and Anne Clarke,
John Shepherd, Keith Harrison and Patrick White.

Stage One

EGG

Scrambled

He's there before morning breaks, before straws
of light can drink up the honey-flaxen
fields. He waits for me to rise with the sun
and then cracks open eggs from the basket.

Yolks slide and ooze into his gaping mouth.
Ribbons of embryonic slime thread down
his throat like strips of slippery sea kelp.
Mucus drips from his chin and he casts eyes

upon me. I wince, turn away, and try
not to gag. I can't bear to see him swallow.
Just like a woman, he says bitterly,
then gulps it down. One day, he tiptoes in

and brings a soft-boiled egg. He tells me
to slip it inside my mouth and hold it.
It's squishy, moist and sits poised on the flat
of my tongue. He says my mouth's the henhouse

and I should keep the egg tucked in my cheek.
I hold it like a secret, careful not
to jiggle or scrape, not to jostle or bite,
but to keep it warm in the dark hollows

of my mouth. He says I'm angelic
with a milk-white egg in my mouth. He says
raw eggs are for men and soft-boiled are for
women. *What about the children?* I ask.

Beaten till scrambled if you tell anyone.

Ode to a Poem

I wrote a poem Neruda would blush at,
Blake would find innocent and Ginsberg
would howl at. The poem was bathed in the plum
shade of an O'Keeffe flower. Imagine,
blooming a poem like that, words perfuming
the body in one delectable scent-
ence after another. I wrote the poem
last winter before the snow, or perhaps
it was September, ripe and red as the wood
stove pushing heat up the smokestack to pant
hot spurts into the starry sky. The poem
had no heart, soul, or glass to shatter it.
There were no carnal apples or oranges
sliced, but it quivered like a grove of aspens.
No poem—not even the sallow sunflower
dripping seeds from its black eye, not even
the weight of a song—could compare. The poem
—not this one—was the best poem ever written,
and when I read its sublime words out loud,
there was a silence unheard of till then.
I wish you could have heard it. The poem
fractured time and space. Each word splintered
the bone-white page. The poem rose like a ghost-
ship out of water, breaching the surface
like a whale caught in a bohemian fog.
I wanted to share that poem with you
today, but the poem had a previous
engagement and sent me in its place.
Great poems can do that. Poets can't.

At the Circus

He says elephants can hear a rainstorm
a hundred miles away and when they come
upon the bones of their dead they nudge skulls
and tusks with their trunks. They never forget.
What I recall from under the big top
is the elephant ride Dad put me on.
The elephant plodded slowly, swaying
like water, leaving footprints like unlit

moons across the dirt floor. I remember
feeling foolish, as if he had left me
naked in some department store window.
The animal lumbered on, so painfully
slow that not even the dust stirred beneath
his shackled feet. I was riding atop
a saggy mountain, world tinted gray,
weaving like a Winnebago through winter.

When the ride ended, I rushed off without
saying a word to anyone. I wish
now I'd taken the time to look, to touch
to give thanks. I never heard the air shift,
the clouds darken or the rain fall before
it hit the ground. What's left is the memory
of my father and that elephant going
in massive, silent circles to please me.

Time of My Life

That summer I was Frances Houseman
learning to tango, samba and meringue,
giving up leg warmers and off-the-shoulder

slouchy sweatshirts for white canvas tennis shoes,
cut-off jeans and spaghetti-strap tank tops.
In the mirror, I made my 'hungry eye' look,

batting butterfly lashes and sipping
kisses from soda bottles labeled Sam,
Dalton and Johnny. I'd ascend the stairs

in Mother's heels, stuff my bra with tissue,
and swivel my hips like a bar stool
at the Double Deuce. It was the year my heart

went *gagoom* for the boy in the slick black
pants who could mambo, cha-cha and salsa
me right off my clumsy, flat-footed feet

Maybe, if I had found an Indian-
head penny, taken up a potter's wheel
or said 'ditto' more, I might've had a ghost

of a chance. Mostly, I was the crybaby,
the wallflower wilting in the corner,
the girl carrying the watermelon.

God's Gift

The mystery did not lie in the fruit
but in the fig leaf she placed in paradise.
She was able to capture the figment

of his imagination, the apple
of his eye. She strutted her garnished self
down the garden runway, a shimmering

peacock in the rising heat. She didn't fret
about panty lines, thongs or brief encounters.
She wasn't crucified by bone corsets,

nettlesome nylons or satanic spandex.
She had it perfect in the beginning.
She turned over a new leaf and blew

his God-fearing mind to kingdom come.
She knew he'd want to peel it off, nibble
flesh and plant seeds at her core. She knelt down,

waited for the dust to settle and smirked.
She knew she could rise above it, had faith
she could figure out how to fabricate

good soles for her to-die-for snakeskin boots.

Waste Not, Want Not

For Sherin Mathews, who was found dead in a culvert
after her adopted father force-fed her milk

Consider everything—the small space
between bones and teeth, cracks of light, hollows
of darkness, calcium and cartilage.

Contemplate whether the glass is half-full
or half-empty, whether to weep if milk
spills in moonlit rivers across a floor?

Somewhere a stove pot froths at the lip
and boils over and somewhere it soothes
a wee one's cry. If the cup were brimming

with twilight, the stars could flitter like fire-
flies and burn holes through the blackness. Maybe
someone thought the milk was spoiled and poured it

down the drain, not knowing it could catch
in the pipes and clog. If the milk were left
to stand it might've grown skin. Even something

seemingly sour can turn sweet again.
In the dead of night, coyotes take nips
at the moon and the details film over

like a half-digested dream. It wasn't long
ago that kids were found on milk cartons
and folks knew better than to dispose of them.

The Seismologist Cries on Wolf Mountain

The 'Big One' is coming. It's inevitable
as the wave that'll rise from its ashes and split

like an atom over us. They've been drilling it
into our heads since childhood to drop to the floor,

take cover and hold on. Not even a couplet
can hold it together when a stanza of earth

breaks from the verse of the world. We know it's bad
but we giggle when we shelter under our chairs.

Some of the bigger kids think the 'Big One' will suck
us down the drain like a flushing toilet. Experts

warn that when we stop shaking, we'll have seven
minutes to reach higher ground. My eyes quickly climb

to the tippy top of the tallest pine tree
and I wonder if kids will have time to crouch.

Will they close their eyes like storm shutters or cry
openly? Surely no one is laughing now.

Maybe the fault lies within. Perhaps there's too much
stress on our plates. In the end, I see a mountain

of empty desks and chairs, piled high to the sky,
and running below it is a river of cell

phones calling out: *The person you're trying to reach
is unavailable. Please try again later.*

The Wheelbarrow

There is no rain-glazed wheelbarrow here,
only chickens by the white cottages.
Someone must've taken the wheelbarrow.
God knows, it was shiny and new, candy

apple red and gleaming with beaded drops.
It certainly wasn't the kind of wheel-
barrow one should leave out in the rain
—when clearly so much depends on it.

Would it have fared better painted a slick
canary yellow or a sleek parrot green?
What about the rusty chickens? Perhaps
the girl with the plump and tender breasts

inside the cottage would prefer to eat
a salad. Maybe she doesn't want to
see a chicken strip. Maybe she went cold
turkey after it left a foul taste

in her mouth. Surely if the barrow were found,
she'd have to catch the chickens, wheel them
down to the water's edge and then roast them
over a fire by the white cottages.

For the Birds

Ever see a bird trapped in a building,
the frantic swooping about, the banging

into windows, the unclear exits?
Mostly they go unnoticed, a gray fog

of feathers lifting up to the rafters
only to sift down like snow without a branch

of light to land on. With each passing hour,
the bird becomes more erratic, less bird,

more stone. It zigzags across the room,
smashes into a wall and then falls

like a cloud over a clear mountain lake.
Oh, to be so wild and then so broken!

Make what you will of this: I let him in
and closed the door swiftly behind him.

It's All About the Yoga

A forest of women are stretching their leafy green limbs
to the matted, mossy floor. They are ferns
unfurling branches, bending and arching
their newfangled bodies with open minds.

I'm the camel plodding along, sweating
it out in the dry hump of midday.
I don't belong here in this dense grove
of women, this cathedral of ever-

green composure. I don't wear a red
cape, drive a blue minivan or drink wine.
I am a trinity of all three
melting into a twisted rendition

of Edvard's *Scream* in an ugly frame
of mind. I am not sitting lotus
or posing as the fallen angel.
I'm the woman in the yoga pants,

downward dogging it to pick up toys,
warrior lunging through the grocery store,
and upward facing the television screen
till I undertake the corpse position.

Snapshot

This is a picture of
me as a child—
with my mother and father.

Slightly out of focus
are the Indian paintbrush,
the lavender lady's slipper,
and the baby's breath.

If you could see past the white space
no one looks at, you'd see the light
refract off its glossed-over edge.

You'd see the sharp stones
in the pocket of my white dress,
the gun behind my father's back

Spoiled Rotten

Imagine the crack of light from the fridge
spilling over the dark side of her face
as she leans in to find you've left her

a single egg in the vast emptiness.
At first, it seems harmless enough, lying
there in the blue glow, a planet alight

between the mountainous ridges and peaks
of cardboard. She sets it on the table
and in one fluid motion swipes the egg

from its dull corrugated galaxy
and sends it orbiting down the cosmic
runway of the table. The egg teeters

at the edge and then craters to the glazed
granite floor with a satisfying splat.
This isn't about the egg or the carton

it came in. It's merely a way to mask
the fleeing metaphor like a bandit.
No one wants to be the last rotten egg.

Stage Two

CATERPILLAR

Applesauce

You were a good dancer, knew all the steps
till we ended up in the back seat
of your dad's Fairlane and you got cold feet,

leaving me to take the lead. I forged
ahead, fingers foxtrotting, quick, quick, slow,
down your chest to your soft underbelly.

I could smell the sharpness of leather mix
in with the mustiness of your damp skin,
It was hot that night, like that one summer

the air was thick with flies and manure.
I had snuck to the cellar to cool off
among the forbidden jars of peaches

and applesauce. Forgive me. It felt so good
going down there. The peaches were heady
and ripe, juicy and firm in sweet nectar.

Peaches bruise easily when taken like that.
With you, it was more like applesauce.

Good Girls Don't Bleed

For Kiran Gandhi, who ran the 2015
London Marathon without a tampon

Shame on you for not being more discreet
and sanitary, for not dressing it up
as Aunt Flo, Cousin Ruby and Uncle
Tom. You must've known there would be fallout,

that papers would spatter your blood-soaked tights
for the whole world to see. This is not
The Sisterhood of the Travelling Pants!
What made you think you could go with the flow?

Women have spent years covering it up,
veiling it in darkness and pretending
it doesn't exist. Who bloody cares
that you trained for a year? What gives you

the right to run by the seat of your soiled
red pants? I've been to the segregated
classrooms, seen sculpted-pink interlocking
parts pulled from plastic nesting vaginas.

I have felt the humiliation
of my discharge from the uterine
army. You leaked out our secret and now
we'll be on the run forever. They may

confine us to huts, burn us at the stake
and call us evil. I watched you cross
the finish line, your bright face beaming
like a full moon, your pants singing my shame.

Cougar Pie

When preparing cougar pie, fresh cougars
are best. Check your local diner or mall.
Cougars tend to lounge outside laundromats,

supermarkets, and neighbourhood pubs.
Once captured, keep cougar in a cool place
until ready to use. Warning: Declaw

cougar and let simmer. To prepare: Place
cougar on table, counter, desk or floor.
Any flat surface will do. Cougars

are tamer when tenderized. Some cougars
can be tough, so it's important to choose
the right one. Leaner is a good choice,

or trim the fat first. Cougars taste
heavenly with the bone left in. You might
feel inclined to give it a good pounding,

but this will cause bruising. Cougars respond
well to being kneaded, preferably
with the hands, until tender. Rub with soft

strokes, working from the centre out, drawing
the flesh to the bare edge. When you've given
one side a good once over, flip it

and repeat. Be careful. Don't be overly
enthusiastic. Your goal is to massage
the meat, making it easier to chew.

Once pliable, lather liberally
with oil and wine and leave it to stew
in its juices. Cougar pie tastes great

with multiple fillings. Drizzle your pie
in chocolate, honey or mango sauce.
Serve cougar pie warm, topped with thick cream

that's been whipped until stiff. Bon appétit.

Hit the Road, Lumberjack!

It was the hairiest of times. It was
unbearable at times. It was the age
of red flannel shirts, dark denim jeans
and knitted chin sweaters. The lads looked

like mountaineers, sailors and lumberjacks
yet didn't scale cliffs, navigate the sea
or have an axe to grind. They ascended
the corporate ladder, boarded cruise ships

and stayed in their cabins. Outdoorsy meant
catching phishing scams, pirating movies
and getting hacked by trolls. Gone were the days
of lanolin soap and straight-edge razors.

The only foam they saw was the white froth
on their frappuccino cups. Men were half
the face they used to be and united
they hunted the five o'clock shadow

to extinction. They unleashed their inner
yetis and why in the dickens not?
There were no close shaves with cougars, not one
hair out of place on their chinny chin chins.

Academy for Girls

At the friday market in Fahaheel
a man follows me with a wheelbarrow.
I pass Turkish rugs, Arabic teapots,
bolts of velvet, watered silk and muslin.

I smell perfumes, spices and potpourris.
I settle upon a mosque alarm clock.
It's white with gold minarets and it belts out
the morning and evening prayer.

When the men pray, their spines curl like crescent
moons. The same men who are called to pray call
me: Eahira: American white whore.
I reply that I am Canadian,

but I'm nameless as Lot's wife, a pillar
of salt left standing in a welt of sand.
I have no language to speak of, no faith
in the devout women who brought me here.

I follow the warm henna fingers of wind
home and set my alarm clock on my desk.
I watch for its small hands to cup its face
and then forbid it to pray anymore.

Canehdian Jesus

The stories would change. Noah would build a sled,
Daniel would face a den of wolves and Joseph
would sport a fur coat of many hides. Christ
would sail past a clothesline of rocky mountains

pinned beneath the white cotton clouds and breeze
into the Hudson Bay where he'd trade in
sandals for snowshoes, crown of thorns for a toque
and a robe for a parka. We'd welcome him,

offer up our spirits, moonshine, and toast
pints of honey maple on tap. Imagine,
his surprise at seeing breath stir like smoke
and finding out that walking on water

wasn't such a miracle after all.
He might give us the cold shoulder, pray
for a chinook and duck out of the Last
Supper. In the end we'd apologize,

tell him to take it up with God and then kill
him anyway. We already know there's no
looking back. Even God knows this is where
Hell froze over and Heaven cracked open.

What's Between Us Is This

Space

dark matter
that makes up
billions of particles
that neither of us
can see.
You sit on the sofa
and gaze over
at me on the love seat.
It might as well be
an ocean   or desert
between us.

Behind us is the fire-
place which holds the frame
of us, our wedding
inanimate
as the mantel
we stand on.
You wear black
and I wear white.
We face each other
but again this

space

this ever widening gap
that grows like rings on water,
rings within trees.
You can't always see them
but deep down
you know they are there.

Carving

I am the housewife
in a housecoat
watching the sun rise and set
on an unmade bed. An unmade
woman. An unmade mind.

I am the midwife
lost in the blue
fibres of lint long picked
clean, pared down
like the skin of an apple
in the stainless steel sink.

I am the butcher's wife,
shaved and lean
with tenderloins wrapped
in blue velvet.

He's the butcher,
far too busy chewing
the fat to notice.

Snow in the Sahara

The day it snowed in the Sahara
is the day you left us. Honey-

amber dunes morphed into the white knuckles
of mountain peaks. As the snowflakes fell,

you dropped F-bombs across the house,
sending the kids running for cover.

In the Sahara, the sandman slept
under a blanket as Bedouins

pressed footprints into snow, slid down
Creamsicle hills and built snowmen.

Before you walked out I threw a chair
and a hot bowl of chicken noodle soup.

It was unexpected—like the snowfall
in the Sahara, fire and ice colliding.

The Birthday Party

I should've asked for his last name, taken down
his plate number and made a mental note
of his distinguishing features. Instead,

I sent her on her way with a gift bag
full of pink tissue paper and glitter.
When she doesn't return at dinnertime,

the door of my throat slams shut and my breaths
become sharp and jagged like the switchblade
I keep stashed in my underwear drawer.

An hour later, my frosty mind ices
the cake with her barrelling down some cliff,
bobbing in some river or keeled over

in some deep-seated ditch. I check traffic
reports, light candles and pray she comes back.
When they return late in the evening,

I want to punch the man square in the face,
beat him like my pummelled-up heart. Instead,
I thank him, close the door and then go through

the motions of putting my child to bed,
my child who jabbers on about all the fun
she had and I want to slap her—but don't.

Plato and the Pepsi Challenge

Plato frowns up at me from the pages
of an old textbook I'm reading. He looks
the way one might think: chiseled nose, sculpted

eyebrows, marble eyes with no pupils.
True to form, he scowls when I crack open
a Pepsi. My soda hisses and snakes

into the garden of Athens where I see
Plato, holding up a can of Cola
like it's an Olympic torch, proclaiming

that nothing beats the real thing! I find it
difficult to swallow what fizzles up
and then falls flat on its fickle face.

He thinks Pepsis are like poets: phony
reflections of divine perfection.
Perhaps Plato should look in a mirror.

One could argue he's the carbon copy
of another philosopher. Good old
cottage cheese and heart disease pop to mind.

If Plato would step aside from the joke
side of life he might see I'm not the waste
of a new generation. I know

without a shadow of a doubt he'd rise
to the challenge and sip from the fountain.
He'd slug that Pepsi back and then mutter:

What happens in the cave, stays in the cave.

Blue Light Special

I take no pleasure in telling you this,
but simply put, you've become obsolete
and I've pre-ordered your replacement.
He should be here first thing Monday morning.

The good news is I got him at half-price
and I found a model that looks just like you
used to. He comes with a full head of hair,
hazel eyes and a chest like Hercules.

Of course, he doesn't have your sardonic
wit or your uncanny ability
to overheat and shut down completely,
but he's fully loaded with that 'new man

scent' and is triple-guaranteed to come
without defects. His equipment is safe-
guarded from viruses, infections,
and his outer core is scratch resistant.

As you already know, good men are hard
to find and you've become unresponsive,
have difficulty getting started
and refuse to even connect with me.

Please try to remember that I held out
for as long as humanly possible,
but it was a time-limited offer
and deals like this don't come along often.

Stage Three

COCOON

Romeo, Romeo, wtf?

Where's the stout woman peeling potatoes,
the short-haired damsel slicing cucumbers
and the gal bent over the garden patch?
Where's the bunions, the fannies, the varicose

veins and where have all the vaginas gone?
Are they locked in some tower without hair?
Love is not blushing brides, rosy-red cheeks
and ruby lips. It's not about passion

fruit, peaches and melons, cherries popping
from the trees while ripe bananas go limp
and brown. It's seeing past the watery
silks, slithering skins and forbidden fruits.

Love isn't dying. Love is strolling through
dog shit and liking it. Love is not you.
It's me and I'm over it. Dear love poem,
if I call you Romeo, would you come

up for a night cap? I'll pour. You drink first.

Matrimonial Cake

The honeymoon is over and now I hurl
things at your head for impact. I usually miss
the mark but make a point. Other times I punish

you with silence, sprawl out on the sofa
till I choose to make up our bed. When the mood strikes
I list off all the things you've done to hurt me,

lay it down like bricks between us and then stare
blankly at the wall like it's the frame
of our future—dark, cold and unforgiving.

I have to admit I've defended myself
with lines from chick flicks, peeled out of the driveway
for dramatic effect. I've picked up the phone,

laughed heartily into the receiver
and then made romantic dinner plans
with the dial tone. Other times, I've left

the yellow pages opened up to divorce
lawyers, my computer screen on Match.com,
a passport and bikini at the front door. I do

these things because of the matrimonial cake
we served at our wedding. Mother reminded us
of its bumpy top, sweet filling and firm base.

Neither of us remembers how it tastes,
but we both agree there were many dates
and that it crumbled apart in our hands.

In a Rut

When times are lean we head for Alaska,
where he'll fish, trap and hunt, and I'll gather
berries, haul water and tan hides. He dreams
of caribou, moose and bears while I root

for tomatoes, spices and kidney beans.
On his day off, he takes his gun and trails
deer droppings and scrapes out to the forest.
I imagine us off-grid, shivering

in an icebox, our frostbitten bellies
under a chandelier of bones. I wait
by the door and shoo deer away like flies.
When he returns empty-handed, he finds

me beneath velvet light, a madwoman
wildly clipping coupons to save a buck.

When Did You Leave?

You forgot

to write down your schedule.
I saw your empty
coffee cup, your broken
glasses by the breadbox
and your razor
on the table.

Your side of the bed
was rumpled. I smoothed
it out before rinsing
your hair and dander
down the sink.

Your clothes missed
the hamper. I stooped down
and put them in with mine.
I turned off the weather
channel and fired a dark
load into the washer.

When you're sleeping,
I count the syllables,
strain to hear
the whispering verbs
pulsing in nouns.

Sometimes when you're late
I log into your chequing
account to find out
where you are.
Sometimes when you're here

I forget.

Distortion

I'm in love. Not with you
      but with the moment
you hesitated.
      I captured you,
kept you suspended
      on the cedar planks
of the Capilano bridge.
      I know you won't change,
will never enter
      the gaping wound below.
You dangle above
          my watering eyes,
double exposed,
      yet more focused
than I ever could be.
      I love the way you look,
the way your hands flutter up
      like fledglings mid-flight.
It's easy to hold you
      —love this thin can be held
from the outside in.

Idol

Maybe she's bored of being the Blessed Virgin,
being placed on pedestals and pulpits, adorned
on altars and chapel ceilings. She's had enough
candles lit at her feet to burn Heaven down.

Maybe she'd prefer to drape her blue self
over a bar stool and ponder life without
the drapery and hardware. She must be tired
of being hailed like a cab, evoked in the night

and preyed upon by sinners. What she needs
is detox for the divine—to rehab old habits.
I imagine her lifting the veil and falling
like a rain cloud onto a street. She follows

footprints into a watering hole, surrenders
her life preserver and orders a Bloody
Mary. She tries to forget the eternal tides
that moon over her each night. She's fed up with figs

and fish, wants to suck the blue marrow from a rib-
eye steak, dip wings in hot sauce and let devilled
eggs dissolve in her mouth. She doesn't want a man
who makes things from scraps of wood, nor one who totes

nets and tackle. She wants to tremble like wild
wisteria, throw olives into a parched wind
and no longer appear as the nun getting none.
Maybe Mary just wants to be idol no more.

Salmon Run

I never told you but I left you once.
It was late September. I packed the kids
in the car, caught a boat to Nanaimo
and checked into the Coast Bastion Hotel.

It was there I pondered leaving for good.
Even salmon know when it's time to run,
to take that leap up freshwater streams,
to reach their ritual spawning grounds.

They'll risk life and fin for their children
before rotting into ocherish dust.
All night the foghorns wailed in the harbour
like women in mourning and I felt numb

as I sank into the soft-red ashes,
the sweat and dander, the microscopic
bits of love left on the pleated sheets.

There's an emptiness that will reel you in
like a riptide, a whirlpool sucking you
inside while the blue-silvery light swims
out into the tapering darkness.

In the half-light, I bundled up the kids,
followed the long-narrow halls past vending
machines and ice and then crossed the lobby
vast as an ocean with no ships in sight.

Three Minutes

The time it takes to make the bed, grab
a hot shower, boil an egg, fold
a paper airplane. Three minutes. The time
it took my mother to make up her mind

to leave my father. I can still hear
the cap popping off of her Final
Net hairspray, the spurts of air hissing
out and freezing her blond curls into place.

Sometimes winter scars the land, conceals
the lesions and diseased tissue below.
Everything appears so spotless and clean,
almost beautiful in its rebirth,

but if you pull the snow back like a scab
it will bleed. I wonder if the earth aches
when it thaws. Three minutes. The time it took
the doctor to uncross my legs, grab
the cryoprobe and shoot a steady stream

of arctic-blue liquid nitrogen
against my cervix. Three minutes
before a glacier unearthed my body,
once beautiful as unbroken black ice.

The Dilemma

It was never about
whether to eat the grapes
but whether to eat each one
slowly, letting sweet innards
spill against my lively pink
tongue, or take in mouthfuls
and split skins with my teeth
like a sharpened pickaxe.

You did not enter
the equation till long
after they were gone,
and only then did I
surmise your indignation,
from the furrow of your brows
frowning from your forehead
when your fingers reached deep
into the bowl and felt
brown, skeletal branches.

I would blame the goblins....
The goblins did it!
The goblins gobbled the grapes.

They also took the cash
from the bedside table,
the car keys and the wedding
ring you slipped in your pocket.

Steller's Jays

When the Jays appeared, they both stood up
from their wingback chairs and marvelled

at how the birds lit up the reddening
yard. They welcomed them with sunflower seeds,

suet and water until a great flock
of feathers dappled their lawn. The birds pecked

at windows, left droppings and made a God-
awful racket. Frustrated, the couple

nailed up pie plates to the cedars and pines,
planted an owl off the railing and played

yowling cat recordings. They removed
the food and water and even purchased

a BB gun. When the jays vanished,
the couple looked out at their vacant yard,

and in the blue absence, they listened
to the sweetness of air licking its dry-

puckered lips. They closed the drapes and returned
to their wingback chairs, and that, my friend,

is why BB guns are so dangerous.

Full of Crow

She packs crows in her freezer,
wounded black soldiers hard pressed
in crosses and rows. In spring

a flurry of crows takes flight
in her kitchen where she chops
them into piles. She slices off

soft plum heads, plucks violet-
washed wings and snips beaks and claws.
She slits the knife wing to wing,

hooks fingers inside and snaps
open their brittle rib cages.
With ice chests open, she spoons

out rich blackberry centres,
mashes bits of pulpy flesh
into jars and preserves crows

in pectin. Crows taste best on
toast, bagels and honeybuns.
From her roadside stand, a flock

of men, women and children
migrate to where she serves out
a murder of crows, grinning

as they chew bitter sweetness
from the white picket fences
of their dark, ravenous mouths.

Editing an Island

Diving right in, I felt it got off
to a rocky start. My head was swimming
by the third line and I was getting tired

of going in circles. Perhaps people
might connect better with an airport
or a bridge, which reminds me, I found it

a tad dark in places. There were far
too many trees. Maybe if you cut out
some of the forest, it would lighten it

up a bit. A few streetlights couldn't hurt.
Did you sense, as I did, that the shoreline
had entirely too much water? The sand

dollars were drowning in it and the beach
imagery fell flat. The water seemed to
interrupt the natural flow of things.

You might be inclined to include some hills,
a mountain or a park bench to sit on.
It might do you some good to abandon

the small stucco houses, the marina
and seaside pub. There wasn't enough there
to hold it together. Even your fog-

horns and barking seals put me to sleep.
Overall, it felt closed off from the real
world and it moved too slowly for my liking.

The only thing worth keeping was the line
of ferry traffic curled like a comma
around the corner, past the ocean-blue

sign printed with: *One sailing wait from here.*

Stage Four

MOTH

Hide and Seek

It was your favourite game as a child.
You were small and could shape and curl yourself
into all sorts of places. Your giggle
is what gave you away. I once found you

under the coffee table, face squashed up
to the green bevelled glass, your body tucked
and folded neatly below. Your face left
a smudge like a shadow. It's been years since

we last played. Outside the snow bellyaches
soft and blue as flakes of sky fall silent
across a field where once lived a clear lake.
There's a flat line where a fence used to be,

a line charcoalled in crows and geese. Ice curls
a snarled lip around the water's edge.
The air is stone and the grass is rubble.
I can see the frostbitten docks, the quills

and prints. I can even see the shadows
that cast and vanish below. Strangely,
I couldn't find you that day, but today
I could walk to the exact spot. I can

see you under the frosted pane, body
folded beneath with rosy fingers pressed
up to the hard surface, your small white lips
latched to the cold breast of ice above you.

Disc Jockey

I arrive with a playlist, a send off
of songs, mostly Motown. You always loved
The Temptations best. I had picked the last

of the blackberries, had seen the boats hunker
down at Degnen Bay and the gray leaves dent the air.
There were patches of purple vetch creeping

up your legs and an unsung requiem
lingering between us. They say hearing
is the last to go. I want you to know

I was listening. I began the countdown
with 'Ain't Too Proud To Beg', and then played
'The Way You Do the Things You Do', followed

by that song you left on my answering
machine when I was still your little girl.
I hear you gulp back swigs of desert air

as if they were mouthfuls of cold water;
a dying thirst. I leave when the music
fades. The blackberry brambles are bone-dry.

The pears are ready to fall. Back at home
I belt out: 'Papa Was a Rolling Stone',
a last eulogy that embalms me whole.

The Parking Stub

In my car just below the wiper blades
is the parking stub from the hospital,
the one I put there, face up on the dash.

As they rushed you into Emergency,
I drove in circles looking for a place
to park. I have never seen a lot

so full of emptiness. I fed quarters
to the fortune teller who spat out
the date and time of our untimely

departure. It's the slip of paper
I can't part with. It's the last time you held
my hand, my gaze, my heart, my attention.

I left before my time was up, watched
the space open up as I drove away.
I wondered where all the slips ended up,

whether they were remembered or forgotten,
left or taken, lost or found and wondered,
would anyone park here if they knew?

Woodwinds

He's the sound of pine and fir crackling
in a forest, the rustle of salal
berries, ferns and chanterelles underfoot.
He's snow crunching beneath heels and boots,

geese trumpeting above trees and clouds,
and the drizzle of rain off black silk boughs.
He's the thwack of logs pitched into a pile,
the dampening flop of a plaid jacket

and the swoosh of cedar waxwings swooping
as the axe catches green slivers of light.
He's the crinkling leaves, the brushstroke
of branches and the sprinkle of sawdust.

He's the wheelbarrow creaking its way home,
the lumbering footsteps on the dark stairs
and the hiss of a Red Bird match sparking
the air into blue halos of hemp smoke.

This man who scarcely says a word divines
a chore into music. He witches sound
from the woods like it's an underwater
spring that flows a perfect chord between us.

Planet Bingo

I call Planet Bingo to let him know
his mother was rushed to the hospital

and isn't expected to live. He says,
at the bingo hall there's a box full of balls

and there's an engine that produces wind
which makes the balls fly up. It's called the ball

blower, The Ball Blower Automatic.
He used to be called a floorwalker. He's not

called that anymore. I can figure out
why it's not called floorwalker and why it's not

ball blower, The Ball Blower Automatic.
They've got these new one-dollar games they call

Hot Balls and some people don't like saying
'Hot Balls'. It's based on the machine, the ball

blower, The Ball Blower Automatic.
This one time The Ball Blower Automatic

needed cleaning and a floorwalker washed
it and short circuited the whole damn thing!

They had to go all day without the ball
blower, The Ball Blower Automatic.

These are the sort of things that go on
at the bingo hall, he says. He pauses

and I ask if I've called the right number?
He yells, *Bingo* before disconnecting.

In the Metal Ward

He bulges in geriatric spandex shorts,
varicose veins flaming down his calves to gout-
ridden toes braided in Jesus Christ sandals.

His silver hair combs the runways above
his raisin ears and there's a helicopter
landing where his old turf once was. His white

knuckles are ringed with studded spikes and skulls.
King cobras unwind from bleached-out muscles.
He buries his heart beneath a faded

Led Zeppelin shirt. I tell him we're in
the mental ward but he just keeps rocking
his chair—rap, rap, rappin' on Heaven's floor.

The Other Woman

She's younger, slimmer and better looking.
She knows how to bait your eyes with her short
skirts and low-cut blouses, clothes I can't pull
off anymore—but then neither do you.

She's too young to know better, but she laughs
at your jokes and drinks up your words like cock-
tails at the Plaza. I found her lipstick
in my panty drawer, the love letters

scarred in perfume, her name plus yours squiggled
inside of a heart. She's not a stressed-out
mother of two. She's soft hands shaping
dust into mandalas, elephant piles

of gray laundry into sparkling white hills,
and broken dishes into mosaics.
She's Supergirl while I'm Elastigirl
stretched every which way but thin, too weak

and tired to save Mr Incredible.
She's the unspoken friction between us
and a whisper of the girl I once was
before I let the other woman go.

The Aftermath

Marriage is the frying pan
I slugged you with,
the sizzling

bacon grease spitting
hot white scars
down your naked back.

I meant it when I said
till death do us part,
but let's face it,

if we were stranded
on an island
and there were but one

coconut left on the tree ...
Hell, we both know
I'd kill you for it.

Divorce for Dummies

Tell no one!

Not your best friend,
your spouse or your mother

—especially
not your mother.

Do not engage in small talk.

The weather will change.

Don't look in mirrors
and don't look back.

Things are closer than they appear.

Leave the wild goose chase
with the eggs and bumps.

Get a rifle
and go duck hunting.

Barrel ahead

like it's Niagara
                    Falls.

Pretend,

he never saw it
coming.

Things Left Unsaid

When my mother says what she says,
in that way she says, when she's not
saying what she's saying, but saying

it in that way she does, it becomes
a choir of mothers, an ensemble
cast of her copied from childhood

and they're all standing in a row
with their disapproving eyes, saying
what she's saying in unison.

When my mother says what she says
when she doesn't say what she says,
I want to scream all the things

I never had a chance to say.
Needless to say, she is right
when she says what she says, not saying

what she says, but saying it
in a way so that when all is said
and done there's nothing left to say.

A River of One's Own

Virginia, no one will go mad tonight.
The moon's obscured by urban clouds, rushing
down the skyline to cover that bridge
of water, where the blacked-out moon sits hung-

over from drinking another ocean
on the rocks. Virginia, you are the blue
moth of morning, the sapphire wings of dawn
unfolding from the darkness and driven

towards the light. Did you brush the moon dust
from your pale wings? Take to air like a silk
thread and sew up that grey hemline of sky?
Did the River Ouse tremble beneath your feet

or did it sing a song to the sea, letting
your stream of consciousness hum along?
You left your hat and cane by the water's
edge, waded in with a pocket full of rocks

and slipped carelessly through the moon's fingers.
Did you emerge from the darkness to find
a place, however briefly, to rest,
before drowning in that diaphanous light?

Wintering

I'm crouched in the bath when I'm overcome
by a sinking feeling, much like the slow
drain of pigment melting beneath a snow-
encrusted landscape. Under the skylight,

I glimpse a twinkling strand of silver
beneath warm folds of water, like tinsel
tangled in the scrub brush. I'm mortified.
My beaver doesn't give a good gawd dam,

has high-tailed it out of there and has left
a badger to burrow in the dark roots.
Do I pillage the village, torch the fields
in hopes of a better crop? Who'll dine

downtown if there's too much salt and pepper
on the table? Who'll choose shepherd's pie
when there's cherries left to pluck? I don't want
my fair lady-in-waiting to fold up

like an accordion box, a windbag
croaking refrains of 'Roll out the Barrel'.
What I need is a fur trapper to catch
this silver fox that travels these private

parts. I'm hunched in the claw-footed tub
watching my camel toe turn pigeon-toed,
as the old crone from the mouth of the cave
gains a toehold on my clitography.

Acknowledgements

I gratefully acknowledge the support of the BC Arts Council.

Some of theses poems first appeared in *The Impressment Gang*, *The Stinging Fly*, *Rattle*, *In/Words Magazine*, *Outburst*, *PRISM International*, *Claw and Blossom*, *Southword*, *Quills*, *The Journal of Compressed Creative Arts*, *Midway Journal*, *The Blue Nib*, *The Maynard*, *Poetry Pacific*, *Tishman Review*, *Zetetic*, *Oddity*, *Third Wednesday*, *Rat's Ass Review*, *FreeFall*, *Island Writer*, *Big Smoke Poetry*, *The Knicknackery*, *Room*, *Feathertale Review* and *Ygdrasil*.

Thank you to my family, friends, teachers and peers for their support and love—without you, this book could not have been written. A special thanks to Ariel Stewart, Silva Zanoyan Merjanian, Sharon Frye, JT O'dochartaigh and Phillip Larrea for always having my back and always telling me, or rather showing me, how it should be. Thanks to Stephen Guppy, Kevin Roberts and Ron Smith who taught me how to show and not tell.

Thank you to everyone at the Porcupine's Quill who helped make this book a reality. Thank you Tim for the gorgeous cover. A big shout out to my editor, Stephanie Small, who read every word of every line and sent hundreds of comments, edits and suggestions (322 to be exact!). No one will ever read my work as closely as you have! Thank you.